A DOG'S Guide to HUMANS

KAREN DAVISON

with Contributions from Bob the Westie

ISBN 10:1492841951

ISBN 13:978-1492841951

TABLE OF CONTENTS

Introduction

My name is Bob; I am a West Highland Terrier. Recently, Karen Davison gave me first prize in the Impeccably Trained Owner Awards, in her book *It Shouldn't Happen to a Dog Trainer*.

While I have developed some skills in the people training department, I am also fortunate enough to own a particularly malleable human. Some people are an absolute doddle to train; some however, can be a bit more challenging.

The author asked me if I would collaborate in this publication and share a few tips and tricks on how my fellow canines may improve their lifestyle.

Humans are sociable creatures and often live in family groups. Like us, they are intelligent and adaptive, which can make them easy to train, but unfortunately their intelligence can also work against us.

In order to get the best out of your humans, you need to establish what makes them tick. It is a matter of working out which behaviour elicits the best responses, and then use that as a method of getting what you want.

If humans do something, and are rewarded for it, they are more likely to offer you the behaviour again. This is called positive reinforcement training, and you will find tips on how to utilise this method in later chapters. People tend to respond well to this approach.

It is my hope that this book will help you to develop a deeper understanding of human beings; their basic care, exercise requirements and tactics that can be used to get better food, improved sleeping quarters and much more.

At the end of this book, you will find a quiz that will help you to determine your level of expertise as a people trainer.

Woof, woof.

Bob

What is a Human?

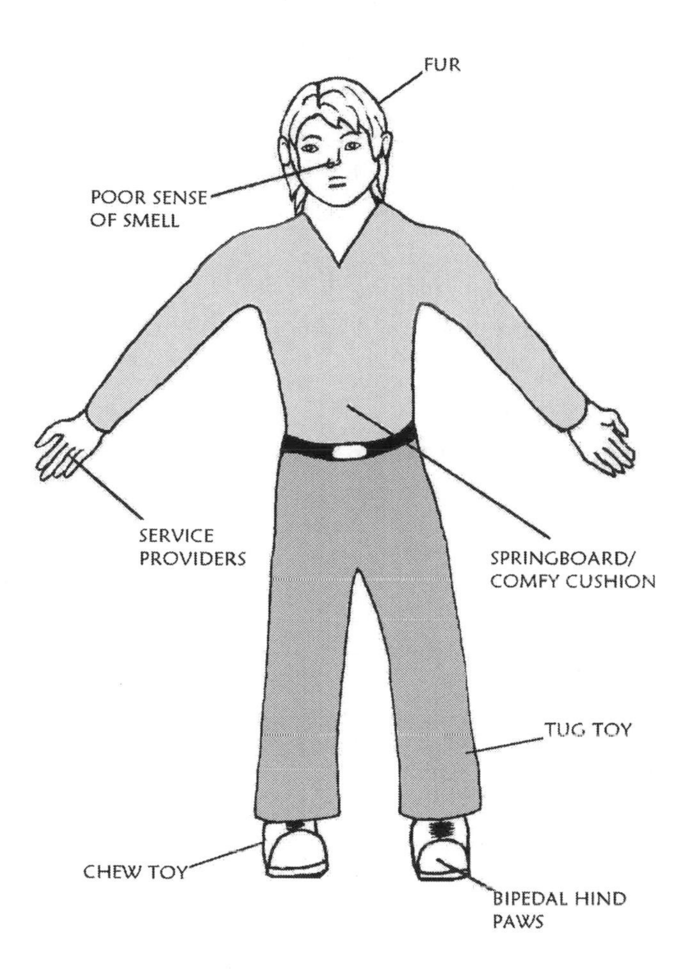

Canines began to domesticate people some 14000 years ago, and over time have developed a mutually beneficial relationship with these monkey type mammals. They are omnivores, and are successful hunter-gatherers, so generally supply bountiful food caches, and usually provide more than adequate dens for us to share with them.

In return, we offer them unconditional love and companionship, as well as many unique skills such as:-

- Territorial marking
- Landscape gardening
- Early intruder alert services
- Personal protection
- Personal fitness training
- Emotional support and cheering up
- Mental stimulation, by keeping 'em on their toes
- Keeping their offspring occupied
- Waste disposal and crumb vacuuming

Human Anatomy

People only use their hind paws for mobility. As this bipedal method of motion is inefficient, they tend to be quite slow, so be prepared to spend considerable time waiting for them to catch up. Their energy levels are quite low as well, so do try to be patient. Having said that, they do need to be exercised regularly, so you will find some tips on how to keep them fit, in later chapters.

Their hind paws are completely smooth and soft underneath, which doesn't afford much in the way of grip, and their toes are small. With this poor design, they have to use over-paw wrappings before venturing outside the den. When you see humans putting these on, it is a good indication that it is time for you to walk them, so keep an eye out for this nice clear signal.

People often have several different paw coverings, the ones that are not in use they tend to leave around on the floor, thus giving us permission to use them for their alternative function, as chew toys. These are handy for curbing boredom when we are left alone, but for some reason, they seem less than pleased when they return and find them dismantled. Go figure!

The fore paws are not used for motion, but are extremely useful tools and provide valuable services, for example:-

- Supplying food and treats
- Stroking and petting
- Scratching behind the ears
- Throwing toys
- Tug of war. (For some bizarre reason they use their paws for this instead of their teeth.)
- Driving the mobile dens used to take us out to the park, beach, woods etc.

As people generally stand upright on their hind legs, their mid section is often exposed. If you launch yourself at this spot from a distance, it makes a fantastic spring board. When humans are in the sit or down position it also doubles up as a warm and comfy cushion.

Humans have poor coats. So poor in fact that they have to utilise removable pelts to keep their hairless bodies warm and provide them protection from the weather. These pelts can be used as readily available tug toys and for getting chase games on demand, which will be covered in detail in later chapters.

Only the head generally has permanent fur, which can vary in colour and length. The males of the species may also have fur on their faces, which can be useful for de-furring your tongue.

Human Senses

The human sense of smell is nearly non–existent; people only have 5 million scent receptors and their noses are dry, which prevents the capture of scent particles. It is hard for us to imagine such limited olfactory abilities, as we have an average of 250 million receptors, it is our most important sense, but people cannot use their sense of smell to interpret the world as we do. They rely mainly on their eyesight and hearing which are not quite as efficient as ours either. Luckily for them, we perform an early territorial intruder alert service; otherwise danger would be sneaking up on them left, right and centre. Makes you wonder how they manage to survive without our help.

To make up for their poor sense of smell, humans do excel in their sense of taste, which is quite impressive, credit where credit's due. People have approximately 9000 taste buds. We on the other hand only have around 1700, so smell for us is far more important to stimulate our appetite than taste. Luckily humans do not generally know this, so they like to give us different foods as they think we get bored with the same taste all the time, so keep that little fact to yourself.

Body Language

This is where things can get tricky. It is important to remember that humans are not dogs. Their body language is different to ours, which can lead to some confusion and misunderstandings on both sides.

To our way of thinking, their greeting rituals come across as rude. People do not appreciate or engage in a mutual exchange of scents as we do. They seem to jealously guard their most informative body parts, and if we attempt to gather scent information from their genitals, they can get rather offended.

Without allowing scent introductions, they will often come straight at you and put their forepaw over the top of your head. This is not meant to be assertive and intimidating; rather it is an affectionate gesture...strange, but true.

Other aspects of their body language can also be a bit odd. For instance, a person can invite you to come over to them in a friendly and inviting way by crouching down, then, as you approach, they stare at you and show you their teeth! One can understand how this might be confusing, but apparently direct eye contact is not a threat and curling lips up and showing teeth, is actually considered a friendly greeting in human circles.

Temperament

Humans are complex creatures. They have a massive array of emotions that we cannot comprehend; consequently they can come across as rather unpredictable. For instance, when we have kept ourselves amused all day re-arranging the garden, instead of reacting with pleasure, they can take you by surprise with their belligerence.

The best approach is to go with the flow. Over time, we have developed an instinct of how to adapt our behaviour according to their emotional state.

When humans are sad or unhappy, silent companionship is the order of the day. They get comfort from us being close, so just be there for them with encouraging, gentle tail wags, and a soft expression. This usually cheers them up.

If you detect that your two legged companion is frightened or anxious, immediately switch to high alert protective mode.

If they are angry with you and showing signs of aggression, it is best to stay out of their way.

Communication

Human beings rely mainly on a complicated set of sounds to communicate with each other. Unfortunately they sometimes expect us to be able to understand what some of these yips and yowls mean, and often get annoyed when we keep guessing wrong. Ho hum.

One valuable tip, if you ever hear the sound 'dog trainer', start psyching yourself up to offer model dog behaviour. This sub species of human, 'the dog trainer', seem to have special powers, it is uncanny how they can suss out even our most cunning and devious tactics. These individuals are not at all trainable, but if you pay attention, they will teach you what some of the yips and yowls actually mean, which is handy.

If the dog trainer visits your den, it is important to pretend that your human companions have exaggerated your behaviour. So when the dog trainer arrives, go calmly over to meet them and sit by their feet, looking up at them adoringly. No jumping up, leg humping, chewing, biting or tugging on clothes.

Do everything that the dog trainer asks of you and while the dog trainer is still there, be obedient and responsive for your humans. Once the dog trainer has left your den, you can go back to normal.

Using your Natural Assets to Influence Human Behaviour

Human beings on the whole, have a natural instinct to nurture the helpless. So one of the most useful and effective expressions for manipulating them is the 'sad puppy' face. This works well, especially with the females, pups and yearlings of the species. It can be used in many and varied situations and is extremely effective for invoking feelings of pity and guilt in people, which you can then turn to your advantage. So use it often.

Another useful expression is the 'happy dog' face. Ears up, silly grin and tongue lolling. This is a good one for letting people know they are on the right track, and for positively reinforcing the behaviour you want to encourage.

The play bow, front end down, bum sticking up in the air and tail wagging furiously is an invitation to play. Most humans understand these positive postures and if you have your training right they should respond in a positive way.

One area where people often misinterpret our body language is when we feel unsure, threatened or intimidated. In this situation we usually offer a clear signal that we want to diffuse a situation and want to avoid confrontation. Ears back, tail tucked between the legs and reduced body posture is recognisable to other dogs as appeasement behaviour. This will usually result in other canines reducing aggression. We are trying to say 'I'm no threat, please don't hurt me' but often humans interpret this as the equivalent of a person looking 'sheepish' so think we are saying 'I know what I've done wrong and I'm feeling very guilty'. This of course is not true, as thankfully we are not burdened with such complex emotions, but often this can cause people to get more aggressive. The more we display submission the more annoyed they can get, which is perplexing. Be a little careful how you use this one.

Exercising Your Human

Humans should be exercised regularly. Taking them off territory is a good way to keep them fit and to provide them with stimulation.

Begin by letting your human know that it is time to take them out, by fetching their lead and dropping it at their feet. If you do not have direct access to the lead, go to the area where it is kept and bark persistently. Some people can be a bit slow on the uptake, so run over to them and bark, then run to the lead and bark. Keep repeating this process, and eventually even the slowest learners will get the hint.

People have certain ritualised behaviour that they need to complete before leaving the house. This can include adding extra over pelts, changing paw coverings, finding keys etc. This can be a tediously slow process, so hurry them along by running up and down, spinning around and barking excitedly. When they are finally ready to leave the house you just have time for a quick chase game, before you allow them to attach their lead to your collar.

As soon as the door is open far enough to get your head through, make a dash for it, moving them along as fast as their two legs can carry them.

In order for you to be in control of the walk it is important that you are out in front. To achieve this, always try to move along at a faster pace than they can manage, keeping maximum tension on the lead.

To keep them on their toes, keep continuously crossing from one side to the other in front of them; this is a good focusing exercise. If they don't pay attention they trip over you and end up falling flat on their face.

It is necessary to let them rest often, so when you find an interesting scent, you can really take your time checking it out while they get their breath back. Refuse to move until you have fully explored the smell and feel that they are sufficiently rested. You can then take off again at a brisk pace.

When you get to the park, you can let them off the lead. You don't have to worry about them as they know their way around, so you can leave them to get on with their walk, while you pursue your own interests.

Given a choice, humans can be rather lazy; they dawdle along at a painfully slow pace. The best way to jolly them along into a run, is to start chasing something that they would consider inappropriate. Here I bow to the superior talents of my colleague, Fenton, the master of human exercise trainers. For those of you who are unfamiliar with his techniques, I refer you to a video of him in action. Go to YouTube and search for *Fenton the dog*. Watch and learn my friends, watch and learn.

While engaging in this three-way pursuit game, humans like to let everyone in the park know your name – they must be so proud – as they shout it out repeatedly. This is a bit of a strange custom, but don't worry, you will soon learn to ignore it. This is when we learn that we have a middle and sometimes even a surname. In Fenton's case, he seems to have four names…Fenton Oh Jaysus Kryste. That is impressive, I think you will agree.

While you may not be as fortunate as Fenton to have access to a herd of deer to pursue, with a little effort and some imagination you should be able to find something to chase. For example rabbits, dogs, people running, people on bikes and there are always the birds…birds are everywhere.

When you have finished having a lovely time chasing your pretend quarry, you may notice that your companion is really lagging behind, and are so out of breath, they are no longer shouting your name. Their body language seems to fold in on itself, and they look smaller and somewhat deflated. This is a good indication that they have depleted their energy levels. At this stage, you can go back and retrieve them, put their lead on, and drag them home.

Home Alone Activities

Often, our two legged companions go away from the den for long periods of time, leaving us alone. Solitary confinement can be so tediously boring, especially when they forget to leave us something positive to do. Obviously, one of our main responsibilities is to guard against intruders. There is usually at least one burglar that attempts to break in. Strangely it is always the same person; they try to gain access by shoving their hands and paper through the hole in the door. They are not particularly brave however, and a good barking and lunging display soon frightens them away. Once this duty has been performed, there is very little else to do, so here are a few suggestions as to how you may curb boredom and pass the time in fun and interesting ways.

Indoor Activities

One area of stimulation is to explore interesting sounds and textures. If you have access, dismantling soft furnishing such as cushions, sofas, armchairs and pillows make a gratifying ripping sound, and usually have some interesting textures to explore inside. To start this off, use your incisors to nibble a small hole to get you started. Use your feet as leverage and keep pulling and tugging until you hear a nice ripping sound. Once you have made a nice big hole in the outer material, you can amuse yourself by stripping out the soft stuffing. It is amazing how much floor coverage you can get out of a small cushion. It makes a much bigger bed than when it is confined inside the cover. Your human companions are bound to appreciate the wisdom of getting more mileage out of the material.

Paper shredding is another activity to pursue to pass the time. To give yourself some variety you can choose between items such as books, magazines, kitchen towels and toilet rolls depending on availability.

Problem solving is another important pastime, and is not only interesting, but often can gain some worthwhile rewards. Working out how to open the kitchen cupboards can be a nice little challenge. Obviously the best cupboard to work on, is the dog treat cupboard. You may have to apply your entire arsenal of problem solving skills for this, which is extremely satisfying and worth persevering with, as the rewards are well worth the effort. If you are unable to actually open the door you could try dismantling it with your teeth.

People bury emergency food caches in bags and bins, so raiding these usually reap many rewards. It might not be much of a challenge if the rubbish is stored in plastic bags, but the contents are many and varied and always worth checking out. Sometimes refuse can be stored in hard bins with lids that are difficult to open. If you have tried and failed to gain access with your nose, look for a paw switch, which is usually in the middle near the floor. If you step on it, the lid opens automatically. If you are still having problems, my advice is to use your paws and your body weight to knock the entire bin on its side, often this results in the lid coming off altogether, allowing you to drag out the goodies.

In between these activities, it is nice to relax for short periods, this is when you need to find something to chew. If there are no toys or dog chews available, you can improvise. Paw coverings are usually readily available, and wooden items such as chairs, table legs, skirting boards and door frames make reasonable chew items.

When you run out of things to do and start getting bored, persistent barking is an effective way of calling your companions home. If you keep it up long enough they eventually hear your calls and return to the den.

Outdoor Activities

Make your human's garden more interesting by indulging in a bit of landscape gardening. You can have hours of fun digging big holes and creating mini hills, while at the same time converting that boring flat space into something much more interesting. This also gives your companions options for putting in the pond they have always wanted, without having to do any hard work. Strangely humans do not always appreciate our efforts.

There are many things around the garden that you can utilise as toys. Plants make good items for throwing, catching, tearing and chewing. The best plants to use are the ones that have only just been put in, as these are easier to dig out. Unfortunately, they are not very hard wearing, so do not tend to last very long, but you can always go and get another one if you are enjoying the game.

Alternatively plants in tubs are a good choice as you can also play with the pots. They make a very satisfying sound when you bite them and shoot off at interesting angles when you pounce on them. Hours of fun right there.

Pulling washing off the line can be entertaining. Larger items such as sheets are a good place to start as these tend to be easier to reach. As you develop your jumping skills you will be able to reach the more challenging smaller items. These make a good gift to present to your human on their return as they are easier to carry. You will be rewarded with their squeals of delight when they see their best bra or undies hanging out of your mouth. They seem especially excited if they have visitors with them. You may even get rewarded with a really fun chase game, but more about this in later chapters.

Training Your Human

Food Training

When humans return to the den after a successful hunt, they arrive with a mouth watering array of goodies. Although people do love us, it seems that they are not hot on sharing their best food caches. We get the dog food.

They believe it is a well balanced and appropriate diet, as it contains everything we need. If it is that good, how come I have never seen one of them eating it?

With a little persistence, a deal of manipulation and a big dollop of guilt trip, it is possible to up your ante in the food stakes.

Stage one, hunger strike. When the dog food is put down, give it a couple of half hearted sniffs, then look up at them with your best sad puppy face. Refuse to eat it, walk away with your head hanging low, not forgetting to pause and glance back at them with your best hang-dog expression. Slump down with a big sigh and turn your face away from them.

Stage two, getting some of their food. There are two different approaches you could employ to train them into giving you people food, depending on what incentive your particular humans work best for.

Method one – when they sit down for their dinner, get excited; put on your happy dog face, run round in circles to show them how excited you are, and bark. You could try using your paws, or sitting up to beg as an added incentive.

Method two – try going under the table, put your head on their lap and look up at them with your most endearing expression. Try not to drool on them if you can help it, as sometimes they can object to this and remove you from the room. It is worth trying your luck around the table with various humans, as some of them are more inclined to take pity on you than others. Trainable people will give you food from their plate. Eat with relish, reward them by vigorous tail wagging and demand more.

If your people do not give you food from the table, you may be able to train them to add some of their food into your dog food. Even if they only add a little to begin with, reward them by eating the whole dinner, including the dog food. This will positively reinforce their behaviour. If humans do something, and are rewarded for it, they will be more likely to offer it again.

Once they are consistently adding scraps to your food, start picking around the dog food and only eat the scraps. Once they see that you are only eating the leftovers, you can usually get them to increase this type of food, until eventually they give up on the dog food altogether.

Sometimes you have to go a little hungry during this training process, but whine, plead and beg every time you see them eating their food, to let them know you are hungry, but still refuse to eat the dog food. Many humans will feel sorry for you and worry that you are starving. This is when they may begin to give you chicken, meat or fish as well as other scraps to get you to eat. This is the result we are ultimately after. When you see them throw the commercial dog food in the bin you know you have cracked it.

Once you have reached this stage of food training, you can get extremely fussy and only accept the foods you like best.

Another top tip for food training is to keep an eye out for people entering the kitchen. Always follow them in and execute your most effective begging methods whenever they open any of the cupboards they use to stash food. One of the best cupboards in the kitchen is the strange cupboard that contains winter all year round, this is where human bury their best food caches.

Advanced training – for the real personal touch some humans can be trained to hand-feed on demand. This is achieved by waiting until you are getting the food you really like, then go back on hunger strike. Many people will try and encourage you by feeding you a titbit from their hand. Take the offered morsel, and if they put the dish in front of you, turn your head resolutely away from the bowl. They will usually pick up another piece and feed it to you. At this stage you nearly have it cracked. From this point on, only eat food when being hand fed. This way you not only get really good food, but lots of nice attention as well.

Play on Demand Training

In this section, we will look at some effective methods to get your humans to play on demand. Given the right incentive, people will engage in all sorts of fun activities.

When you decide you want to play a game, go and find a toy, drop it at their feet and utilising your best happy dog face, bark excitedly. If they are being a bit stubborn, scrape at them with your paw, increase the volume and add in some high pitched yips as an added incentive. Keep picking up the toy and chucking it at them, increase the volume of your bark, until they decide it's easier to play with you, than to put up with the hassle.

Once they have complied with your demands to play, do try to control the game. A wise dog once said 'control the game, control the human'.

As an example, we will look at the game of fetch. When people are controlling the game, they throw the toy, wait until you retrieve it and place it at their feet, before throwing it a second time. This is okay, but you can double the fun, by changing the rules. When we are controlling the game, the person throws the ball for us to chase, but once in possession of the toy, try turning the tables and make them do the retrieving. If they want the toy, they have to chase you, to get it. This is where you need to get your balance right. If you make it too difficult, they will give up; so make them think that they are able to keep up with our superior agility and speed. In reality, we could run rings around them all day, it is highly amusing seeing them floundering about, bless them. But we must give them some encouragement; let them experience success quite quickly to begin with. Slowly, slowly, catchy, monkey.

If you are having difficulty getting them to chase you to retrieve a toy, you can get a similar result by stealing undies from the washing basket.

This nearly always results in a fun chase game. The best time to engage in this game, is when they have visitors in the den. The more people present, the better the response. Take your time routing through the basket until you find a suitable item. Take it straight to the visitors for inspection, throwing it up in the air a few times, so everyone can see your prize. You know the game is about to commence, when you hear your human let out a high pitched screech.

Playing chase indoors is brilliant fun. Humans clutter up their dens with all sorts of obstacles which can be used to prolong the game. One of my favourites is round and around the armchair. If there is only one human joining in the chase, you can keep this going for ages, as they are incredibly slow at changing direction. If by chance they have rustled up a team to help them, then the sofa is a better choice. You might be outnumbered, but you have more room to manoeuvre, and with quick bursts of speed, you will always keep several steps in front of them.

Another good prop is the kitchen table, it is plenty high enough for us to get underneath, but humans are not inclined to drop to all fours to follow. Even if they do suss this out, they are even slower on four legs. You almost feel sorry for them…almost. The table has four posts, which can facilitate some inventive avoidance tactics. When you have had enough of the game, drop the prize. At this point of the game, it is advisable to execute a rapid retreat.

Outdoor chase games are reasonably easy to instigate. In order to encourage them to chase you in the garden, keep an eye on the weather. The most successful time to engage in this activity is after a few days of rain, followed by a nice dry day. In these conditions humans invariably wash a load of over-pelts and bedding and hang them out to dry. Nice clean fresh clothes, suspended over sodden muddy grass. I think you can see where I am going here.

Choose an item carefully; you don't want to pick anything that is too big, as it will get tangled in your legs and impede your movement. Once you have removed a suitable item, make sure you bring it to their attention, by jumping up at the window to show them what you have picked. If they are a bit slow, tap the window with your paw to get their attention. As soon as they spot you, the game is on.

Adding even more amusement to this game is their total lack of grace on this type of muddy surface. They slip and slide in the most ungainly manner, so you may have to stop often to allow them to almost have you within their grasp, before taking off again. Once you have had enough, you can drop the once clean item in the mud and allow them to retrieve it.

Another good game to teach humans is tug of war. The removable pelts they wear are cleverly designed to incorporate tug toys in the form of trouser legs and sleeves. Humans absolutely love this game, they get quite excited, barking and squealing and joining in the fun. Sometimes they flap their arms and legs about to make it even more interesting.

Despite the fact that people have a rather pathetic sense of smell, they can be taught to play find games. A good choice for this game, are the fluffy paw coverings that they wear around the den.

In order to teach them the game, you should make it easy for them in the beginning. Retrieve a slipper and parade around in front of them with it in your jaws, giving it an occasional shake. When they react, take off at full pelt. You should have plenty of time to select your hiding place before they catch up with you. Don't forget that humans are incapable of locating anything by scent, so they will need a lot of help. When they get close to the right spot, encourage them with excited barks to let them know that they are on the right track. When they eventually find it, reward them with vigorous tail wags and licks. Once they are getting the idea of the game, you can start making it more challenging by hiding their possessions when they are not looking. If you can't get access to paw coverings, select an object that they use on a daily basis, otherwise, they might not notice. Some suggestions: the little boxes that control the TV, their mobile talking devices and the mobile den keys.

If you are finding it difficult to train humans to play on demand, then consider your timing for such activities. Take note of their TV watching habits. If you frequently hear a particular theme tune, it's a fairly safe bet that this is one of their favourite programmes. This is a prime time for training as they want to hear the programme, so tend to respond quicker to your demands. This is also a good time to drag out your most annoying squeaky toy and squeeze it repeatedly until you get the desired results. In this circumstance try not to push your luck too much as they are not inclined to leave their seat to chase you, so it's better to return to them with the toy, squeaking it constantly so they will throw it again. Slowly, slowly catchy monkey.

Attention on Demand Tips

Getting attention from humans is one of our favourite things; good, bad or otherwise, we are always up for it. If you feel you are not receiving the attention you deserve, here are some sure fire tips.

One thing that people seem to respond well to is when you jump all over them. This is a great way of getting attention on demand as they nearly always react in a positive way. The rewards you receive depend on the personality type of your particular companion.

Affectionate people nearly always give you a good ol' fuss, or if you are small you may get picked up and cuddled which is rather nice.

Playful people will turn it into a really fun pushing game. The aim of this game is to gauge your response to match theirs. They push you away and you jump back at them with equal force. The harder they push you away, the more force you can put into your re-launch; this is when you can really utilise the spring board effect of the human mid-section. Sometimes they may put their knee up to push you, so not only do you get to push back but you can also grab the offered tug toy and swing off their clothing. This is great fun and extremely rewarding.

Sociable people may start a pack barking and howling session which is always fun to join in with. The more you jump up, the more they bark!

If you are not getting the desired attention when jumping up, look at your timing. You should generally get a reward from even the most unresponsive person when they have their hands full. The most effective time to execute this manoeuvre is when they return home from hunting and are loaded down with food bags.

If you plan this carefully you may even be able to open the bags with your claws in the process, emptying the contents on the floor. Not only does this usually get a good response, if you are really quick you can grab some of the goodies, which can then turn into a really exciting chase game as a bonus.

Persistent barking is another tactic that can result in rewards. Some people seem to enjoy this activity, as they start shouting and barking as well, joining in the fun. Other human beings can be quite intolerant of constant noise, so use this to your advantage. They will try all sorts of things, just to get a bit of peace and quiet. A common reward for barking is a nice hide chew, bone or pig's ear. They give us these to keep our mouths occupied in a quiet manner. So when you fancy a nice chew treat, bark until one is produced. If your two legged companion is particularly malleable, they might play a game of guess what the dog wants, and will offer all sorts of choices until they hit upon one that works. This has endless possibilities, so use your imagination.

You can even use this tactic to gain a better resting place. This is achieved by giving a strong intruder alert bark. Invariably, one of them will get up to see if there is someone there, allowing you to move in and steal their nice warm seat. When they return, make sure you have your most contented and angelic expression, and pretend you are fast asleep. Not wanting to disturb such peace and happiness, they will often choose to sit somewhere else. Obviously do not abuse this, as we have all heard what happened to the dog that cried wolf.

When you want to settle down for a good petting session, the nose nudge under the arm or hand, is a nice clear signal of what you expect. Failing that, snuggle up with them, put your head in their lap (so it is readily available) and look up at them with your most loving expression. Humans are suckers for this one.

Sleeping Arrangements

Surprisingly some people do not need any training at all in this area, as they allow you to sleep with them on their bed from day one. It might be that these people have had some training before. Only extremely trainable people allow this however. In some cases you may have to settle for a comfy armchair next to the heater, which is also a prize spot, with the advantage that you do not get disturbed by fidgety humans.

At the other end of the spectrum are the people who have gone out and brought a dog house for you, thinking that you will be quite happy spending night-time outside in solitary confinement. This assumption is sadly misguided. Separated from the family, all alone in the cold and dark...I don't think so. If you find yourself in this dubious position, don't despair, follow these tips and I am confident that some improvements can be made. These people will need a fair bit of effort to train. As this is quite involved, it is best to break the training down into small stages, in what we term 'shaping' behaviour. The idea of this type of training, is to work in small stages; once you gain success at each stage, you can move onto the next level.

Your first goal should be to get inside the main den. This is where some of your neighbouring canine friends come in handy. Save your energy until all the lights go out in your den and the dens next door; this is the time to begin barking, whining and scratching. You can add some howling for good measure, making sure all your vocalisations are at full volume.

Human sleep patterns are different from ours. If we are tired, we nap, this could be at any time of day or night. People do all their sleeping after dark. In order to function properly they need at least eight hours of uninterrupted sleep, so make sure you are making enough noise so that sleep is impossible. An even more effective approach is to create a racket until they are definitely awake, and then stop for ten minutes. This is just enough time for them to begin drifting off to sleep, at this point, you want to give your sharpest, loudest barks to make sure you jolt them out of it. This can be a highly effective method of sleep deprivation. Trust me, even if they stick it out the first night, they will be like zombies the following day. Not many people can cope with two night's lack of sleep, so persevere.

If there are a few dogs in the area, it is relatively easy to get them to join in, thus keeping the entire neighbourhood awake. Not only will your humans get desperate to get some sleep themselves, but they will be worried about upsetting everyone else, so will eventually give in and allow you into the kitchen. You will be quite worn out after your efforts, so settle down straight away like the good little puppy you are, and don't make another sound for the rest of the night. Your humans will be exceedingly grateful. This is a good example of positive reinforcement, as getting a good night's sleep is an extremely good incentive for human beings.

Once you have wheedled your way into the kitchen you can, after a few nights of rewarding them with peace and quiet, use the same methods to get access to even better sleeping quarters inside the house. If you work diligently you may even get the

ultimate reward and end
up sleeping on the bed with the people.

Rate Your Human Training Skills

Training Quiz

Answer each multiple choice question below, and make a note of your scores.

a) = 10 point

b) = 5 points

c) = 0 points

At the end of the quiz, add them up to rate your skills as a human trainer.

Attention on demand

Q1 When you jump up on your humans, how do they react?

a) Give you a big ol' fuss

b) Push you away or shout/bark at you

c) Ignore you

Q2 If you persistently bark at your humans, what do they do?

a) Play a game of guess what the dog wants by trying all sorts of activities, until they hit on the one that shuts you up

b) Start shouting and barking as well

c) Send you to bed for a time out

Food Training

Q1 When you refuse to eat your dog food, how quickly does your human offer you better food?

a) Same day

b) Second day

c) They only offer you dog food until you are so hungry; you have no choice but to accept it.

Q2 If you are scrounging when your humans are eating what do they do?

a) Always give you some

b) Usually save you a bit

c) Put you out of the room so they can eat in peace

Game Training

Q1 When you want to play a game, how often do your humans comply with your demands?

a) More often than not

b) Occasionally

c) They decide when, where and how long games take place

Q2 When your humans are watching their favourite TV programme and you demand a game, what do they do?

a) Play with you constantly throughout the programme to keep you quiet

b) Play with you during the ad breaks

c) Either take the toy away or put you out of the room so they can watch in peace

Sleeping Arrangements

Q1 When you are dissatisfied with your sleeping arrangements and kick up a racket to object, how quickly do your humans relent and offer you something better?

a) Under an hour

b) At some stage during the course of the night

c) They put their earplugs in and ignore you until you arc exhausted and give up

Q2 When you were first brought home where were you expected to spend the night (before training)? Answer either 1,2 or 3 then move on to the appropriate scoring questions.

1) Outside

2) Kitchen/utility

3) In the bedroom with the humans

What did you achieve after training?

If your answer was 1)

a) Comfy chair

b) Kitchen/utility

c) Still outside

If your answer was 2)

a) In bedroom with humans

b) Comfy chair

c) Still in kitchen/utility

If your answer was 3)

Well done, you score an a)

Score your Training Skills

0-15 points

I feel your pain. I am at a loss to give you any advice, you are either not destined as a human trainer or your two-legged is un-trainable! Your best bet is to allow them to train you, as this might be the only way to get rewards.

15-30 points – Trainer in training

You have some skills but your human is quite tricky, work on the areas that you are getting some small measure of success. Try some of the tips in this book, then retake the quiz to see if you have improved your skills.

30-50 – Intermediate Trainer

Much more promising, this score shows great potential for further manipulation. Keep up the good work.

50-80 – Master Trainer

You either have some serious skills, or your human has had some training before. Either way, you are one lucky pup-of-a-bitch.

Final Note from Bob

It is my hope that you have gained some valuable insights into training your human companions.

If you enjoyed it, please tell your canine friends, and if you are able to leave me a review, that would be awesome!

Please keep your letters and emails coming, I love hearing about your successes and also your problems.

I have been getting a lot of correspondence from all over the world from dogs that are having a hard time, not with our beloved humans, but the old enemy… cats. I will share with you one particularly upsetting letter from Sir Cecil of Indigo Moon:

Dear Bob,
Do we get punished for being naughty in a former life?
The reason I ask is I can't think of anything that I've done in this one, that would result in me being forced to share my den with fourteen cats.
I'm a good boy, or so I'm told, so why is this happening to me?
I can't get any peace, I'm stalked every-where I go.
I daren't sleep, and when I do fall into an exhausted doze, terrible images haunt my dreams.

Last week, I managed to dismantle the fence and break out. I had a taste of freedom, but it wasn't quite what I expected. They are out there as well, in the trees, lurking under cars, hiding in the bushes...

... Luckily the dog warden grabbed me and took me to the pound. In that cold kennel, there were no cats at all!
Finally! I got the best night's sleep I'd had in ages. Sadly my elation was short lived, my pesky microchip gave me away and I was sent back to the den of continued suffering.
I dream of getting a small kennel by the sea. (I heard cat's don't like water) But I need cash.
I've started a GoFundMe campaign:
Sir Cecil's End of Rope Escape Fund.
Any donations would be gratefully received.

Yours hopefully,

Sir Cecil
(AKA Diesel)

Will Sir Cecil get the funds he needs for his great escape? Find out in my new publication. A Dog's Guide to Cats.

We stand united!

Woof, woof

Bob

Other Publications

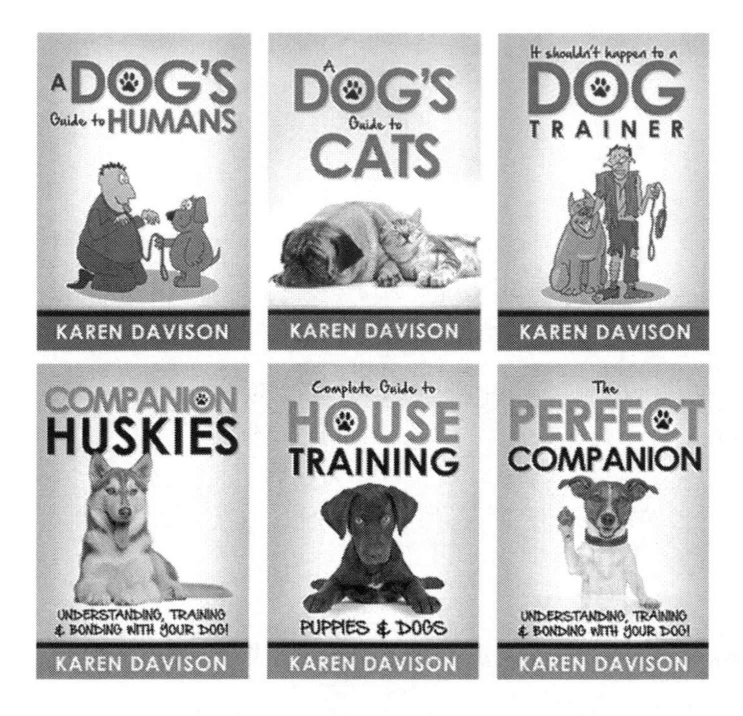

FUN READS FOR DOG LOVERS SERIES

A Dog's Guide to Cats

Bob the Westie once again puts paw to paper to offer a few pearls of wisdom to his fellow canines. This time it's the old enemy… Cats.

Don't be fooled by their apparent small stature and fluffy cuteness, these things have super powers that you can only dream of, and their instincts are as sharp as their claws. Luckily help is at hand

A Dog's Guide to Cats contains all dogs need to get one step ahead of the game, including how to build a cunning trap that will give hours of cat free pleasure!

Packed with vital information, it also includes some heart wrenching and cautionary tales sent in by fellow canines.

Can Bob help them find solutions to their cat problems?

It Shouldn't Happen to a Dog Trainer

Have you ever wondered what ends up on the cutting room floor when watching celebrity dog trainers on the television?

During her career as a professional dog trainer and canine behaviourist, Karen Davison has been battered, flattened, tied up in knots and found herself in some funny, strange and painful situations.

Here she shares some of the 'you couldn't make it up' moments' that have occurred while working with dogs and their owners

POSITIVE DOG TRAINING SERIES

The Perfect Companion, Understanding, Training and Bonding with your Dog!

This book explores the inner workings of the dog's mind to give you a real understanding of how and why, positive reinforcement gains the best and most reliable results.

You will find detailed instructions on how to teach all the basic commands, using various different positive training techniques, so that you can choose the method that best suits you and your dog.

It encourages you to consider your dog's natural behaviour and to channel their instincts into positive activities, and reveals why stimulating your dog's mind, has many behavioural and physical benefits, possibly contributing to longevity. Environmental enrichment and suggested activities and games, will not only give your dog a confident, happy and fulfilled life, it will also strengthen the bond between you, taking your relationship to a whole new level.

Some common behavioural issues are covered in detail, explaining the causes, prevention and solutions, as well as a general problem solving guide, with a checklist to help you diagnose the root cause of problems, and suggests what action may be needed, in order to resolve them.

The Perfect Companion, Understanding, Training and Bonding with your Dog! Written by professional dog trainer and canine behaviourist, Karen Davison, is essential reading for all new puppy owners, and a valuable source of information for those of us, who want to get the best out of our relationship with man's best friend

Complete Guide to Housetraining Puppies and Dogs

Do you need advice on housebreaking? This guide will give you the means to success!

Take the stress out of housetraining and get positive results - fast. A must have guide for teaching your puppy or dog to be clean in the house. With the right approach, house training can be reasonably quick and easy. This guide shows you how.

Topics covered:- Positive approach, effective clean up regimes, first steps to success, training methods, teaching your dog to go on command, diet and nutrition, advantages and disadvantages of neutering, crate training, common mistakes, dos and don'ts.

Companion Huskies, Understanding, Training and Bonding with your Dog!

Combines The Perfect Companion and Housetraining Puppies and Dogs, this book is adapted specifically for this high energy breed and explores all aspects of husky ownership from puppyhood to maturity.

Bonus items, breed information, hereditary disorders, socialisation program and husky sports.

About the Author

Karen Davison grew up in Bedfordshire, England. She has been both an avid reader and a lover of animals since early childhood. When she was eight, the family got their first dog, Scamp, whose great character started Karen's lifelong devotion to dogs.

Since qualifying in Canine Psychology in 2001, she has worked as a professional dog trainer and canine behaviourist. She went on to study Wolf Ecology in 2009 and was lucky enough to spend time with the wolves at the UK Wolf Conservation Trust in Reading.

Her first publication, The Perfect Companion: Understanding, Training and Bonding with your Dog, a comprehensive guide to canine psychology, training and problem solving, was published in June 2012 and won an IndiePENdants' award for quality. Since then she has published The Complete Guide to

House Training Puppies and Dogs, Companion Huskies: Understanding, Training and Bonding with your Dog, and three Fun Reads for Dog Lovers: A Dog's Guide to Humans, A Dog's Guide to Cats and It Shouldn't Happen to a Dog Trainer.

After joining a local writers group, she has spread her author wings and is now enjoying writing poetry, flash fiction and short stories, and after taking a course in screenwriting has just completed her first radio drama script. She is currently working on her first work of fiction, which combines her love of writing, wolves and fantasy - Wolf Clan Rising which is due to be published 2017, under pen name K.D. Phelan.. You can find an excerpt of Wolf Clan Rising at the end of this publication.

Karen is now living the dream, she resides in a country cottage on the west coast of Ireland, drawing inspiration for her writing from the peace and beauty of her surroundings where she shares her life with her husband, two daughters and nine special needs pets. Her seven rescue dogs and two rescue cats have a mixture of emotional, behavioural and physical disabilities

One of Karen's favourite sayings: 'Saving one dog will not change the world, but surely for that one dog, the world will change forever.'

Meet the author, join Karen on Facebook:-
https://www.facebook.com/SmartdogBooks

Coming Soon from SmartDog Books

WOLF CLAN RISING

Book One

K.D. PHELAN

For generations, men and wolves have formed an alliance. Companions and hunting partners, the clan and the pack have formed a special bond, but it is breeding season and wolves are free spirits.

Despite being surrounded by family and friends, Andrik feels alone. His wolf has gone, to return in summer with a new mate and offspring to strengthen the bloodlines. To Andrik, summer seems an age away.

The mage's dreams are haunted by a dark spirit. It moves through the forest, its limbs, tentacle like and writhing, turn everything to ash.

It is a warning, but what does it mean?

Laya knows, she has seen it in a dream that is not a dream. There are strangers in the forest… and they are hunting wolves. A boy travels with them, born into slavery in a city far across the ocean, he had never questioned his fate, but the forest has stirred something deep inside him. Will he have the courage to betray his masters to save the wolf?

The invaders won't stop until they have stripped the land and enslaved its people. With the help of magic can the clans prevail?

Or is this the beginning of the end for the hunter-gatherers?

Excerpt - Wolf Clan Rising

Prologue

Excerpts from the diary of Edian Wright first officer of The Explorer.

Year 712, Moons 4th, Day 29

After many delays, we finally depart Lyconia. The excitement of starting our adventure is tinged with trepidation. We are going into the unknown.

The Emperor committed some of his own personal wood reserves into building this great ship, in the hope that we will discover a new land, rich in much needed resources.

If the bird experts are right, there is land out there somewhere, they have observed birds migrating south, disappearing from our shores for many moons. They must be heading somewhere.

Birds, it seems, are to be our guides. We have brought ravens with us to aid our search; we will release them periodically and from a higher vantage point their horizon will be far beyond ours. They are unable to land on water so if they return to ship, we will know that our search continues, if they spot land, we can track their course.

We have 163 souls on board consisting of 85 crew, 30 craftsmen, 45 slaves and 3 bird handlers. We leave on a prosperous wind on course South by Southwest.

Year 712, Moons 5th, Day 25

After six days, the storm has finally abated. Six of our crew lost overboard, good men all, and Petra's injuries are so bad, the Doc doesn't think he is going to make it.

The storms we had previously experienced navigating the shores around Lyconia pale in comparison to the ferocity and duration of storms out here in the midst of this vast ocean. At least for the time being the sea is calm, and we have made repairs as best we could.

There was great excitement among the bird handlers this morning when they caught sight of an unknown and impressively large seabird. I paused in my work to join them, and the sight of such a magnificent creature took my breath away. The wingspan was wider than the tallest of men, its flight pattern, they told me, was unlike anything they had every seen. It glided effortlessly, using the great expanse of its wings to harness the wind, as it rose and fell, turning and soaring above the waves.

Year 712, Moons 7th, Day 5

We have been away from port for three moons, rations are low and tempers short. We released a raven this morning, and hope surged as we watched it heading away from ship. We adjusted our course to follow, only to find a rocky outcropping, home to thousands of gulls, their raucous cries filling the air, their excrement turning the rocks white. This bitter blow pushed some of the crew over the edge, a fight broke out between two of the men and the Skipper put them both under the lash and cut their rations for two days.

Moral is at an all time low and there are murmurs of dissent. If we do not find land soon, I fear we will all die out here.

The Skipper still has us on a course South by Southwest.

Year 712, Moons 7th, Day 15

Late afternoon we spotted whales breaching the waves in the distance, and over the course of the day we saw patches of weed floating on the surface of the water, good indications that land may be nearby. At first light we will release the ravens again.

These latest sighting have given us some small hope and stirred in me a deep yearning. What I wouldn't give to feel land beneath my feet once again!

Year 712, Moons 7th, Day 16

The morning broke eerily calm, not a breath of wind to fill our sails, the creaking of timbers and the faint lapping of water against the hull the only sound in the thick sea mist that surrounded the ship, cutting us off from world.

It was mid morning before the sun and wind finally cleared it away and we were able to release one of the birds.

We watched as it circled the ship, gaining height and instead of returning, set off on a direct flight path two points off the starboard bow. The skipper ordered a course change and we followed. When we lost sight of it, we released another raven, until at last a great shout from the crow's nest of Land-Ho.

The rejoicing on board was something to behold, even the captain joined in the celebrations, breaking open his last barrel of malt spirit to share with the crew. There are no words to express the atmosphere of joy and excitement.

And what a land! It is more than we could ever have dreamed.

As we navigate its coast it appears uninhabited, with no signs of civilisation, a green jewel of rich forests and vast mountain ranges. A land of plenty, a paradise.

Chapter One

The setting sun filters through the forest, casting golden rays that dance with the spirits of the living canopy. Through the dappled sunlight, a lone wolf moves on silent paws along the narrow trail, his powerful legs cover the ground at an easy trot.

Far to the north, the distant howls of stranger wolves carry to him faintly on the wind; he pauses, pricking his ears towards the sound. Licking his nose he inhales to explore his surroundings.

The north east wind brings with it the scent of snow from the high peaks and the freshness of the White Water river. Close by, rain and earth, the souls of trees, and spirits of a myriad living things that inhabit the forest. The wolf smells what is and also, what has gone before. The older scents are fainter, like the tracks of ghosts.

He registers this in a few heartbeats then lifts his muzzle and flaring his nostrils, casts his mind out further still, seeking the one scent that has caused such restlessness. The one that surrounds him, an invisible force that pulls him further and further away from his pack.

The scent of the she-wolf.

On the wind, a minute trace of what he seeks causes his heart to race. He lifts his head and raw emotion flows from his lips, quietly at first, rising and falling until the air is filled with a long and wavering howl. Caught by the wind, it travels through the forest.

Away to the south his own pack add their song, their voices weaving around his, wrapping him with warmth and comfort, and bringing with it an overwhelming sense of loss.

In the midst of the voices, he hears his soul brother calling to him. His chest tightens and for a moment he looks back over his shoulder but as twilight descends, the faint cry of the she-wolf beckons him north.

Made in the USA
San Bernardino, CA
07 December 2017